SNUC

By
Mike DiSalvo

Uproar Theatrics

LICENSING & PRODUCTION INQUIRIES
Uproar Theatrics, LLC.
hello@uproartheatrics.com | www.UproarTheatrics.com

SNUC copyright © 2021 by Mike DiSalvo

SNUC is published by Uproar Theatrics, LLC
500 8th Ave FRNT 3, #1714 New York, NY 10018

ISBN: 978-1-968051-09-9

First Printing, May 2025

CHARACTERS

Andy Martin, early 30's, Tulane Medical Student.

Kevin, med student and Andy's best friend.
Dad, Andy's father, a worrier.
Various Doctors

Chief Tyler, Head of Oncology at Tulane
Hannah, Andy's older sister.
Mom, a calm balance to Dad.
Alex, a bartender near med school.

Three-Actor Option

Actor One: Andy Martin

Actor Two: Kevin, Dad, Various Doctors

Actor Three: Chief Tyler, Hannah, Mom, Alex

With special thanks to Jason Hedden, whose own creative connection to the Martin family first made me aware of Andy's story. I like to think Mrs. Dempsey would be proud...

ACT I

A medical lab - Tulane University, New Orleans, 2005

Darkness. Outside we hear the roar of ferocious winds, and the pounding of rain. Maybe the distant sound of a siren. There is some serious weather happening.

A door opens in the blackness and light spills into the lab. Silhouetted is Kevin, a med student. His arms are full of books and magazines. He tries to flip on the lights with his elbow, but can't quite reach. He steps into the room and the door swings shut, leaving him and us in darkness again.

KEVIN

Shit.

He moves tentatively in the dark for a moment, and then we hear him bump into something, hard.

KEVIN

Ouch. Shit.

And then he drops all his books.

KEVIN

Shit.

Eventually he finds his way back to the door and flips on the lights. The lab is bathed in a stark white light.

1

*The entire back wall is a huge white board,
used for projections and for writing/drawing with
dry-erase markers.*

*On one side of the lab is a series of cabinets,
shelves, and counters containing various
equipment and books. On the other side is a
large medical freezer and more lab equipment.
Out of place among all this is a typical college
mini-fridge.*

*Center stage is a lab table. On one half of the
table is a microscope, a few notebooks and pens
and such. The other half of the table is set for
dinner: candles, glass of red wine and wine
bottle, and a half-eaten plate of food.*

*Lying face down on the table is Andy Martin. He
is a 30-something med student with a dark wool
cap on his head.*

Kevin sees Andy and smiles.

KEVIN

Dude.

Andy doesn't move.

KEVIN

Dude, you fell asleep again.
> *(He begins to pick up the books and magazines
> he dropped.)*

Also, and I know you know this so it's not like I have to say
anything, but if Chief Tyler catches you with food in the lab
she will flip her shit. I'm talking full-scale, stage four,
Exorcist head-spinning levels of shit. Which, I'm not gonna
lie, I'd kinda like to see, but still...

(He has by now stacked everything on the counter. He turns back to Andy.)

KEVIN (CONT)
Okay. Don't say I didn't warn you.

At this point, Andy's silence and stillness are a little concerning.

KEVIN

Dude?

Kevin steps closer and gingerly pokes Andy with a finger. Andy wakes suddenly, almost in a panic, and Kevin jumps a mile.

ANDY

Huh????

KEVIN

Ah!!!!

Andy gets his bearings while Kevin gets his breath.

ANDY

Wha...?

KEVIN

Dude.

ANDY

Sorry.

KEVIN

Not. Cool.

ANDY

Yeah... sorry.

KEVIN

Dude. I was like, "Uh-oh!" You know?

ANDY

Uh-huh. What were we...?

KEVIN

You fell asleep again.

ANDY

Right. Sleep.

> *He raises an arm against the starkness of the*
> *fluorescent glow*

ANDY

Man, that light is...

KEVIN

Oh, right. Sorry.

> *Kevin moves to a dimmer and lowers the lights.*

ANDY

Sorry, my eyes are still pretty sensitive.

KEVIN

Totally. My bad.

ANDY

It's all right. That's why I brought the candles. Thought it
would be a nice change.

KEVIN

And here I thought you were gonna wine and dine me.

> *Kevin finds matches. He lights the candles. The*
> *two sit in the soft glow for a moment.*

KEVIN

Are you okay? I mean, you seem...

ANDY

I'm fine. Just lost track of time.

KEVIN

You take your meds today? You got that sunken-eyed ghost thing going on.

ANDY

Yeah. Yeah... I just, y'know.

KEVIN

Yeah.

ANDY

Did you bring those magazines?

KEVIN

On the counter, yeah.

ANDY

Cause we may need to think about a new environment, you know, in case...
> *(He looks over at the medical freezer.)*
...and I read about some wild new media with interesting growth factors they were using at...Sloan, maybe?

He stands but is clearly not feeling well. He sways for a quick second, then sits back down, coughing.

KEVIN
You know, we don't have to do this tonight.

ANDY
No, I want to.

KEVIN
Yeah, I know, but you're looking pretty... shitty.

ANDY
Thanks.

KEVIN
Plus, man, it is coming *down* out there.

ANDY
Still?

KEVIN
Yeah. Campus is pretty much deserted.

ANDY
Evacuation orders tend to have that effect.

KEVIN
Was it an order? Felt more like a suggestion to me.

ANDY
If you want to head out I won't blame you.

KEVIN

What?! That hurts! We are in this together. Besides...
(crossing to the freezer and gently petting it)
...how could I leave all the little fuckers? Answer: I couldn't.
I would not.

ANDY

You'll be a great parent someday.

KEVIN

Yo! Please don't lump me in with the procreation crowd, I
am not mature enough to handle that.

ANDY

Sorry.

KEVIN

Accepted.

> *There is a loud gust of wind and a surge of rain.*
> *The two look upward, then at each other.*

ANDY

Maybe it'll blow over?

KEVIN

Not for nothing, dude, but if we lose power? No bueno.

ANDY

I know.

> *Kevin notices Andy's half-eaten plate of food.*

KEVIN

Hey, is that mac 'n cheese?

ANDY

Yeah.

KEVIN

Sweet.

ANDY

It's probably cold.

KEVIN

Even better.

ANDY

Gross.

KEVIN

Says you.
(a thing they do)
Things that are better cold: go.

ANDY

Ice cream.

KEVIN

Funny. Um...
(thinks)
Pizza.

ANDY

White wine.

KEVIN

Chinese food!

ANDY

Seriously?

KEVIN

Aw yeah, man. Delicious.

ANDY

You're disgusting.

KEVIN

No sir, I am a college student.
> *(taking a sip of the red wine)*

Mmm, that tastes like a... red.

ANDY

Very perceptive.
> *Kevin is trying hard to enjoy the wine.*

KEVIN

Yeah... no. I want to but I can't.

ANDY

So young and uncultured.

KEVIN

Uncultured my ass. I can't help it if I have a more refined
palate than you.

> *He walks to the mini-fridge and takes out a can*
> *of Mountain Dew. He takes another wine glass*
> *down from a shelf and pours the soda into it,*
> *swirling it around and then taking a sip.*

ANDY

Good year?

KEVIN

Always.

Andy laughs, which leads to more coughing,
which seems to sap his energy.

KEVIN

We really don't have to do this tonight.

ANDY

We really do.

KEVIN

C'mon, Andy--

ANDY

The money people are supposed to visit next week, right?

KEVIN

Right.

ANDY

We have to be ready.

KEVIN

We are ready. As ready as we can be until, y'know, we have
something to show.

ANDY

We'll have growth by then. It's the last step. Once we do,
then we'll need the funds to take the research to the next
level.

KEVIN

I'm with you man, I am. I mean, it's not like we can have the
Chief set a World Record every time we need more money,
but there's no point in pushing through tonight if it's gonna
totally do you in. Figuratively. Besides, if this damn storm
doesn't let up we might have to reschedule anyway.

ANDY

I thought we were through the worst of it?

KEVIN

I mean, how would I know? I've basically been living in this lab with you for the last week.

ANDY

The spouse I never wanted.

KEVIN

Who else would put up with you?

ANDY

You're the only one.

KEVIN

Exactly. I know some areas have lost power, but the Med Center here has plenty of backup, so... What do you say? Cross our fingers and push on through?

ANDY

It's worth it to take the chance.

KEVIN

You sure, now? If you're tired we can totally--

ANDY

I said I'm fine, can we move on?

>*Kevin sips his soda and considers Andy. Finally, he shrugs.*

KEVIN

Okay, cool. Lay it on me.

ANDY

Sorry?

KEVIN

Your speech. For the money people. Lay it on me.

ANDY

Ah... I don't know, I haven't really thought about that part.
I'm not so good at talking to people.

KEVIN

He says, talking to a person.

ANDY

You know what I mean. Asking for things... I prefer to revel
in self-sufficiency.

KEVIN

Yeah, I noticed that, Mr. "I'm-gonna-do-cancer-research-on-
myself-because-no-one-else-will."

ANDY

I let *you* help.

KEVIN

And my soon-to-be-graduating ass thanks you. Now gimme
your speech.

ANDY

Kev--

KEVIN

Lay it on me!

> *Kevin hops up on the counter. Andy looks at him
> for a moment, then sighs. He manages to stand.*

                         ANDY
Dear... all that have gathered?

                         KEVIN
I'm sorry, what?

                         ANDY
Right. Yeah. Okay.
                  (beat)
My dearest--

                         KEVIN
No.

                         ANDY
Beloved--

                         KEVIN
Uh-uh. Nope.

                         ANDY
Honored...colleagues...?

         Kevin shrugs. Good enough.

                         ANDY
Honored colleagues. Thank you for taking the time to listen
to my sales pitch.

         Kevin groans, but Andy pushes on.

                         ANDY
This kind of research doesn't happen in a vacuum, and
certainly not without the generous support of people such as
yourselves. Like any road you travel that is unexplored,
eventually you come to a point where you simply cannot go
on without help. And that is where we find ourselves today.

Lights dim on Kevin. Andy turns and addresses the audience.

ANDY

As a teenager I was obsessed with my "legacy." What was I going to contribute? How would I leave this Earth a better place than I found it? Lofty thoughts for a man of seventeen, I know, but still... it's probably what drove me to apply to medical school.
(beat)
Four years ago I was diagnosed with a very rare form of cancer. Suddenly the time I had left to create something of importance was much shorter. I was camping with my sister, we were halfway up a mountain, and the view was...

There is a clap of thunder and a roar of wind. The lights on Andy fade.

HANNAH (OFF)

Andy!! Wait up!

<u>On A Mountain</u>

Andy springs across stage, imbued with a new and youthful energy. From around the far side of the wall comes Hannah, Andy's older sister. She has a large crashpad strapped to her back and a hiking backpack in her hand. She is pretty out of breath.

HANNAH

Holy crap, I'm dying.

ANDY

You're not dying.

HANNAH

I may be dying, but only because...
(she tosses Andy the backpack)
...I'm carrying all the stuff! What the hell, Andy?!

ANDY

Sorry.

*Hannah struggles to wriggle out of the
crashpad, at one point getting temporarily
stranded on her back.*

ANDY

You look like a beached Picasso tortoise.

HANNAH

I don't know what that is, but bite me.

*She eventually frees herself from the crashpad
and sits there, panting.*

HANNAH

I don't know why I let you talk me into this. I never realize
how out of shape I am until I go climbing with you.

ANDY

Climbing? That was just hiking. We have not yet begun to
climb!

HANNAH

Uh-huh.

ANDY

And actually, not to be technical, but we're gonna *boulder*,
not climb.

HANNAH

Sure. Whatever. I can't wait. Really.

ANDY

Hannah, come on! I mean, will you take a look at that rock!

HANNAH

Yeah, it's... something.

ANDY

It really is.

> Andy stares in wonder, and Hannah stares at
> him.

HANNAH

Tell me again why we had to make camp three miles away?
There wasn't anything closer?

ANDY

Yeah, I know, there's an odd lack of hotels inside the park.

HANNAH

Bite me again. Okay.
> (She reaches into the backpack and pulls out a
> chalk bag and climbing shoes)
Tell me one more time how all this works?

ANDY

Simple: chalk goes on your hands, shoes go on your feet.

HANNAH

I think you got me the wrong size, these are way too small.

ANDY

They're supposed to be small, helps you grip the rock.

16

HANNAH

That's not what my hands are for?

ANDY

Probably best to use both, just to be safe.

HANNAH

I will most definitely fall.

ANDY

Naw, I'll be right behind you.

HANNAH

What?! No way am I going first!

ANDY

Look, you're gonna be fine. Would I lie to you?

HANNAH

You're my little brother, isn't that kinda your job?

ANDY

Job perk, more like. That and taking money off your dresser.

HANNAH

Jackass.
            (she looks at the mountain)
So... what were you saying about the three points of
contact?

ANDY

Oh, now you're interested?

HANNAH

Now that I might fall off the side of a freaking *mountain*?
Yes. Yes, I am.

ANDY

Relax. It's pretty simple.

> *Andy goes up to the wall, on which there are
> several handholds we can't really see from the
> audience.*

ANDY

The whole idea is that you always want to have three support
points.
> *(He reaches up with both hands, nimbly pulling
> himself up so that one foot rests on a ledge and
> both hands have a grip)*

Two hands and one foot. Or...
> *(he moves, demonstrating)*

One hand and two feet.

HANNAH

And if I should slip?

ANDY

Crashpad!

> *Andy lets himself fall onto the crashpad,
> grinning.*

HANNAH

Yeah. So, I'll be in the bar.

ANDY

Aw, come on! I won't let you get over your head. I'm safe. I'll
be right here the whole time. Also, we have the crashpad.
Also... you're like, barely ten feet off the ground, if you even
make it that high.

HANNAH

I feel like this might be the appropriate time to tell you that I hate you.

He laughs. He pulls himself back onto the wall so that he is holding on by two feet and one hand.

ANDY

Wanna see a deadpoint?

HANNAH

A what?

Quickly, Andy pushes upwards with his feet, reaching his free hand towards a ledge that seems just out of reach. He almost catches hold, but doesn't quite make it and drops back to the crashpad.

ANDY

Damn.

HANNAH

I'm sorry, that's not exactly earning you any trust from me.

ANDY

Worth a shot.

HANNAH

A shot at a dead...?

ANDY

It's called a "deadpoint."

HANNAH

How reassuring.

19

ANDY

Sorry, climbing jargon. It's when the next handhold is just
out of reach and you have to push up to grab it. Ideally, you
wanna be right at the peak of the move, right at that spot
where you may not get there, and then... you catch hold.

HANNAH

Scary.

ANDY

Yeah. But exhilarating, too.
(Beat. He looks at the mountain.)
I like the exactness of it all. You have to plan and plot,
dissecting your way across the rock. Calculating what the
next move will be, where the next edge lies with just enough
room for one toe, and will it be enough to support you? To
get you to the next step? But when you do make it to the top,
and you finally get an unfiltered view of the sunset you spent
all day chasing...
(lost for a moment, he sings softly)
"I am... I said."

Beat.

HANNAH

Um... what?

ANDY

Sorry. That's what usually runs through my head when I'm
climbing.

HANNAH

Bible verses run through your head?

ANDY

That's not the Bible. It's Neil Diamond.

HANNAH

You're sure it's not God?

ANDY

That's "I am what I am."

HANNAH

Oh.
          (quick beat)
Neil Diamond isn't God?

ANDY

Depends who you ask.

HANNAH

"I am...?"

ANDY
          (really belting it out)
"I am, I said! To no one there!"

HANNAH

Dude, are you...?

She mimes smoking a joint. Andy laughs.

ANDY

I promise, I'm not.

HANNAH

Cause I swear to God, Andy, I swear to Neil Diamond, if you
got high and dragged me up a mountain...

ANDY

Um, if I remember correctly, I'm not the one who got busted with pot in their bedroom.

HANNAH

Please, that was one time. It's not like I'm a drug mule.

ANDY

And Dad freaked out.

HANNAH

Of course he freaked out. That's what Dad does.
                    (beat)
Neil Diamond?

ANDY

Don't you remember Mom playing it on car trips as a kid?

HANNAH

Must've blocked it out.

ANDY

I loved that song. I used to make her play it over and over again, and I would think, "Yeah, Neil! I am! I am here, I exist!" You know?

HANNAH

Sure, why not.

ANDY

It's a really great song.

HANNAH

Isn't that the one where he sings about the chair not being able to hear him?

ANDY

(singing again)
"And no one heard at all, not even the chair."

HANNAH

Do you ever sit around and wonder why you're single?

ANDY

Not really, no.
        They laugh.

HANNAH

So. Which route are we taking?

ANDY

No, no, no. We don't call them routes, we call them problems.

HANNAH

Enough with the jargon!

ANDY

Which problem are we going to solve!

HANNAH

I can think of one I'd like to solve right now.

ANDY

Okay, okay.

HANNAH

Please tell me there will be wine at some point on this trip?

ANDY

Chilling at the campsite as we speak!

HANNAH

Thank you, Lord.

ANDY

Things that pair well with Chardonnay: go.

HANNAH

Fish?

ANDY

We're having trout tonight.

HANNAH

Garlic?

ANDY

And a butter sauce.

HANNAH

Not falling off this--

ANDY
(fingers crossed)
Call it a rock.

HANNAH

--not falling off this mountain and dying today?

ANDY

Sorry, you need Cabernet for that.

HANNAH

Worth a shot.

> *Andy laughs and picks up the backpack to move*
> *it out of the way. Something inside catches his*
> *eye.*

ANDY

I'm sorry, why is this in here?

He pulls out a pillow.

HANNAH

Look, I don't know what goes on between you and "the rock," okay? I figured, maybe there would be down time. Who knows.

ANDY

How are we related?

HANNAH

You'll have to ask Mom and Dad.

ANDY

Yeah?

HANNAH

I'm not saying you look like the mailman, but... Andy catches a whiff of the pillow.

ANDY

Man, do you just dowse yourself in perfume before you go tosleep?

He sneezes.

HANNAH

Hey, that is my natural scent, and I'll need it to fight off your little brother stank in the tent tonight.
            (she laughs, taking a moment to look out)
It is a beautiful day.

She stands there for a second. Behind her, Andy has the pillow pressed to his face and has stepped away and doubled over. She turns and sees him.

HANNAH

Stop smelling my pillow, it's creepy.

Andy pulls the pillow away, and the lower half of his face and the pillow are covered in blood.

ANDY

Something's wrong.

A roar from the storm.

Doctor's Office

Andy crosses and sits on an exam table, wiping the blood from his face with the pillowcase.

A doctor enters, face buried in a chart.

DOCTOR

Okay, Mr. Martin--

ANDY

Call me Andy.

DOCTOR

--it would seem, Mr. Martin--

ANDY

Andy.

DOCTOR

--that we found an extremely large tumor in your sinuses.

Beat.

ANDY

Just like that?

DOCTOR

Obviously not just like that, Mr. Martin--

ANDY

Andy.

DOCTOR

--there's no exact way of measuring how long the tumor has been there.

ANDY

Really?

DOCTOR

But the good news is that we've managed to stop the bleeding.

ANDY

That is good news.

DOCTOR

For now.

ANDY

Come again?

DOCTOR

Look, Mr. Martin--

ANDY

Call me ANDY!

The Doctor finally looks up from his chart.

DOCTOR

Yes. Andy. Look. You are in perfect health. Non-smoker,
excellent physical condition. It was probably the altitude that
forced the nosebleed, otherwise it might have gone
undetected for a while longer. I've only encountered a tumor
in the sinuses one other time.

ANDY

See a lot of nosebleeds do you?

DOCTOR

This close to the mountain? Quite a few, actually. I've
probably done two of these a week for the last 20 years.

ANDY

That's 2000 procedures.

DOCTOR

It is.

ANDY

And only one other tumor like mine?

DOCTOR

Not exactly like yours. The other was a benign mass. What
you have is very rare.

ANDY

If you know it's rare then at least that means you know what
it is, right?

DOCTOR

I know of it, but I've never personally dealt with it before.

Andy sticks out his hand.

ANDY

Extremely rare tumor, nice to meet you.

DOCTOR

Andy--

ANDY

I knew I was in trouble when you started in with the "Mr. Martin" stuff.

DOCTOR

I think--

ANDY

If everything had been fine you would have just sauntered in, "What's up, Andy? Had yourself a little nosebleed there, huh? Next time don't climb so high, all right buddy? And thanks for staying away from cigarettes, those things'll kill you."

DOCTOR

What you have is a very rare and highly aggressive neoplasm. Unlucky, I'm afraid.

ANDY

No shit, Doctor.

There is a loud crash, and a roar from the storm. The Doctor exits.

Lab

Andy is back in the lab. He looks at us.

ANDY
The doctors didn't know how to characterize what was
growing in my sinuses. All they knew was that there was a
very large "something" there, and that it was cancerous. So,
they did what doctors do when faced with something
vaguely known yet obviously dangerous... they blasted me
with chemo and drugs. And one year later...

Living Room

Andy's Mom enters across stage.

MOM
(excited)
Andy, are you serious?

Andy crosses to join her.

ANDY
That's what they said, Mom.

MOM
You wouldn't mess with me? You know I hate that.

ANDY
C'mon, Mom, not about this.

Andy's Dad joins them.

DAD
What words did they use, *exactly*?

                           ANDY

Dad...

                            DAD

I mean it. Tell us exactly what they said.

                           ANDY

They said, "Well, Mr. Martin--"

                            MOM

Oh, you hate that.

                           ANDY

I really do.

                            DAD

Just say it!

              They look at Andy expectantly.

                           ANDY

"Mr. Martin, you... are... *cancer free.*"

                            MOM

Oh, honey.

                            DAD

Thank God.

              They pull Andy into a tight embrace. Then Dad
              breaks off.

                            DAD

The Malbec!

MOM

Yes!

DAD

A celebration!

Dad goes to look for the wine.

ANDY

Mm, Malbec.

MOM

Oh, should we wait for Hannah?

ANDY

She doesn't get in 'till tomorrow.

DAD

I am going to toast my cancer-free son, and when my daughter arrives tomorrow we will toast him again.

MOM

But you told her?

ANDY

Called her on the way back from the hospital.

DAD

I'm still mad you wouldn't let me go with you.

ANDY

Yeah, I know, but there was no reason to think the news would be this good this fast. After all, they still don't have a name for what I had.

MOM

I think "cancer" is a pretty specific name.

ANDY

"Cancer" is actually pretty general, Mom. There over five different types of breast cancer, for example.

MOM

Yes, thank you, Dr. Andy, but I think you know what I mean.

Dad has found the bottle. He pours three glasses and hands them around.

DAD

No more cancer talk. I don't want to hear that word in my house again. It has been banished.

MOM

Dear.

DAD

I mean it. Banished.

MOM/ANDY

Banished!

DAD

To Andy. You fought, you won. To getting back to...

He chokes up, unable to finish.

MOM

To Andy.

DAD

Yes. To Andy.

ANDY

Love you guys.

They clink glasses and sip the wine.

ANDY

Man...

DAD

Right?

ANDY

That is good.

MOM

Mm-hm.

They enjoy the wine and the moment.

DAD

Say it again.

MOM

Dear.

Andy laughs.

ANDY

Cancer-free.

DAD

Amazing.

ANDY

Actually, I think they said, "The treatment was successful, no evidence of cancer remains."

MOM

I'll take it.

                            DAD
Me too.

                            MOM
And you're sure you want to go back to school?

                            ANDY
Absolutely.

                            MOM
Because if you need, I mean, if you want more time to relax,
you could always--

                            ANDY
Thanks, Mom, but Tulane said I was still eligible to accept
my place there, and, you know...

                            DAD
That was the plan before.

                            ANDY
And that's still the plan.

                            MOM
All right. But you know, anytime you want...

                            ANDY
I know.

          Dad is looking at the wine bottle.

                            DAD
Hon, do you remember where we got this?

          Andy sneezes.

MOM

Bless you.

ANDY

Thanks.

MOM
(to Dad)
Argentina, wasn't it?

Andy coughs a little, and then sneezes again. He turns away, fishing in his pocket for a handkerchief.

DAD

Bless you again.

ANDY

Thank you.

Andy raises the handkerchief to his face.

DAD
(to Mom)

We tasted it first in Argentina, but I don't think we brought any bottles home with us.

MOM

Oh. Well, we probably just bought it through that wine of the week club the kids signed us up for last Christmas.

DAD

That's not nearly as good a story. We should tell people we bought it in Argentina.

                            MOM

Backpacking in Argentina.

                            DAD

Even better.

> *They notice that Andy hasn't turned back*
> *around.*

                            MOM

Andy, honey, do you need a Kleenex?

> *Andy turns around. There is blood around his*
> *mouth and nose, and the handkerchief is stained*
> *a dark red.*
>
> *Mom and Dad look at him silently for a moment,*
> *and then exit. Andy turns and looks out at us.*
>
> *Behind him, projected on the white wall:*
>
> *"SINONASAL UNDIFFERENTIATED*
> *CARCINOMA"*
>
> *He grabs a marker and writes under the*
> *projection:*
>
> *SNUC*
>
> *He pulls off his wool skull cap, revealing the*
> *bald head of a cancer patient. He slouches*
> *slightly, the weariness and disease taking over.*

                            ANDY

Just like that, it was back. It was all back. The doctors, the
tests, the sad little sideways glances from the nurses drawing
yet another tube of blood. But this time, finally, they were

ANDY (CONT)

able to give my cancer a name: Sinonasal Undifferentiated
Carcinoma. My good friend, SNUC. Almost always fatal,
and as of now only 100 or so cases have ever been
diagnosed. Just to brighten things a little further, because of
the insidious nature of the pathology of SNUC, even a wide
excision of the entire tumor harbors no promise of a cure.
No, no, this one likes to hide. It likes to find hidden and
quiet parts of the body to avoid detection. You think you
have it beat, you are declared cancer-free, and then... when
you least expect it... You know it's bad when you have an
"insidious" form of cancer, for Christ's sake.

KEVIN

Really?

*Lights come up on Kevin, still sitting on the
counter.*

ANDY

No good?

KEVIN

I mean, I appreciate the darkness you got going on, but
maybe try to spread a little sunshine for the people whose
money you are trying to acquire.

ANDY

You're probably right.

KEVIN

It's a good start, though.

ANDY

Thanks.

KEVIN

In other news: Do you think I can pull off a mo-hawk?

ANDY

I'm sorry?

KEVIN

For the big "shave-a-thon." I'm trying to decide what my
new style should be.

ANDY

God, is that really happening?

KEVIN

Hell yeah it's happening. People are excited. It's gonna be
huge.

ANDY

Look this isn't an after-school special, just because I lost my
hair...

KEVIN

It's not that! You look really cool bald.

ANDY

I mean, I appreciate the intention, but--

KEVIN

Dude, will you just let people support you?

Beat. Andy smiles.

ANDY

Can I do the shaving?

KEVIN

Absolutely! Phil already bought a special set of clippers. We
can set you up center stage and let you create follicle
masterpieces on the dome of your choice.

ANDY

There's a stage?

KEVIN

I mean... there should be!

ANDY

It will be nice to know I'm not the only whose head is
freezing this winter.

KEVIN

Cuz it gets so cold here in Louisiana?

ANDY

You know what I mean.

KEVIN

Hardly ever. But... dude, it's gonna be awesome. Jimmy D is
gonna shave an amino acid sequence into the side of his
head.

ANDY

Nerds.

KEVIN

You have no idea. *Also*. I think there are a few girls willing
to do it.

ANDY

Really?

KEVIN

Yup.

ANDY

Which ones?

                              KEVIN
Jill? The T.A. From Infectious Diseases?

                              ANDY
Wow.

                              KEVIN
I think it's gonna work on her.

                              ANDY
We'll see.

                              KEVIN
Women who are sexier bald: go.

                              ANDY
Uh...

                              KEVIN
Natalie Portman in that Vendetta movie.

                              ANDY
Demi Moore in *G.I. Jane?*

                              KEVIN
Classic.

                              ANDY
Sinead O'Connor?

                              KEVIN
Who's that?

                              ANDY
Seriously?

KEVIN

Hey, I'm not as old as you, remember?

ANDY

How can I forget?

KEVIN

You can't. I won't let you.

Andy smiles, shaking his head.

*Kevin hops off the counter. He lands in a thin
puddle of water which sends up a small splash.
He and Andy look at the floor in amazement.*

KEVIN

Um...?

ANDY

Is that...?

KEVIN

Water? Yeah. Yeah, it is.

ANDY

Well, that can't be good.

KEVIN

I'm thinking no, it probably isn't.

ANDY

Where is it coming from?

Kevin walks in a little circle, splashing water.

KEVIN

I mean...

The door opens and Chief Tyler, a woman in her mid-40's, enters.

CHIEF

Okay, gentlemen, I believe that was our cue.

ANDY

What's happened?

CHIEF

Did you fall asleep again?

ANDY

Yeah, but only--

CHIEF

Guys, it's a category five storm system, and it's still coming down out there.

KEVIN

Out there?? It's coming down in here!

CHIEF

Really?

Kevin stomps around some more, splashing water.

KEVIN

I mean, not down, but we got a leak somewhere.

CHIEF

That's not good.

KEVIN

Thanks, Chief Tyler, we already deduced that much.

                         CHIEF
Doesn't matter. We'll have to let it go. Start packing up.

                         ANDY
No, wait, I was gonna--

                         CHIEF
You heard that crash a little while ago?

                         KEVIN
Figured it was thunder.

                         CHIEF
Try the levee.

                         KEVIN
Doing what?

                         CHIEF
Breaking.

          Beat. This sinks in and it isn't good.

                         KEVIN
So...?

                         CHIEF
We have to move.

                         ANDY
Not necessarily.

                         KEVIN
Andy--

CHIEF

Andy, there is water in the lab. There is water outside, there
is water everywhere! I am not sure why we still have power,
but--

ANDY

We have backup generators.

CHIEF

Which will be of no use if they are underwater.

KEVIN

Man, if the water shorts the freezers, then all the samples in
there will be on a countdown--

ANDY

And that's all of me that's left to work with.

CHIEF

Circumstances being what they are--

ANDY

Chief, I don't think I'm up for another round of tissue
excision.

KEVIN

He really isn't, Chief. I mean, look at him, he's--

CHIEF

Enough!
          (Beat)
Look, I know you were hoping that tonight would be the
night we see movement, but we do not have the luxury of
sitting around the lab--a lab that appears to be sinking, by the
way--while the world comes down around us. We have to get
ready to move. Now.

Beat. Andy nods.

ANDY
Sorry, Chief. You're right.

CHIEF
Trust me, you'd rather it was me calling the shots than the National Guard.

KEVIN
Are they here?

CHIEF
Not yet, but they could be soon. If you think I am intimidating--

KEVIN
Naw, not you.

CHIEF
--then imagine me as a 250 pound man in uniform with a gun.

KEVIN
And thank you for that mental image.

CHIEF
Kevin, I swear to God--

KEVIN
(hands up)
I'm done. Sorry.

Andy hasn't moved from the lab table. The Chief walks over to him.

CHIEF

I know what this means to you.

ANDY

Yeah.

CHIEF

When you first came to me, I said "No."

ANDY

You said, "Hell no."

CHIEF

I did.

ANDY

What changed your mind?

CHIEF

Just bored, I guess.
(she allows a small smile)
The work will still be here. I promise. We'll get it done. But now we have to think about you. Okay?

ANDY

Yeah.

CHIEF

Good.

> *She walks to the door. Kevin is staring at her intently and she notices.*

CHIEF

Stop picturing me as a man with a gun.

KEVIN

I'm sorry, I can't!

The Chief leaves. Kevin moves quickly to the door and calls after her.

KEVIN

If it's any consolation you are really making it work! In my head, that is! Really!

(he turns back to Andy)

She hates me.

Andy is staring at his microscope. After a moment, he calmly walks to the freezer and takes out a case of tissue cultures.

KEVIN

Dude?

ANDY

You can go.

KEVIN

I mean, I think the idea was that we both--

ANDY

I'm staying.

KEVIN

You're what?

ANDY

Tonight is the night. I'm taking a look.

KEVIN

Hey man, I understand--

ANDY

Do you?

> *Beat.*

KEVIN

No.

ANDY

I gave up hope that this research will ever be of any value to me... to me specifically. The Chief once asked me what winning would look like. I'm getting... I just... I need them to grow. Soon.

> *Kevin nods. Andy turns back to the table.*

ANDY

If you're going, go. Otherwise, find some towels or something and see if you can keep the water from getting anywhere it shouldn't.

KEVIN

Like the lab?!

> *Andy puts on plastic gloves, arranging the cultures. Kevin looks around. He moves over and opens a cabinet, taking out a few medical towels.*

KEVIN

Perfect evening for it, if you ask me. I mean, we have wine, and candles. Mother Nature to set the mood.
> *(A gust of wind and he looks upward)*
A dark and stormy night, and shit.

> *Kevin is laying the towels down at the base of the counters and the door jam, trying to stem the*

flow of water into the room. He stands there,
watching for a second and then takes a step.
There is a splash of water.

KEVIN

Huh.

ANDY

Mother Nature will not be denied.

KEVIN

Screw her. Tell you what, I'm gonna try the janitor's closet
down the hall. You get the little fuckers ready, and when I
get back... it is on.
(he calls to the cultures)
You hear me, you little fuckers? It. Is. On.

Kevin leaves. Andy allows himself a small sip of
wine. He flips on the microscope. At the same
time, the white wall behind him is illuminated.

From off, we hear a voice.

ALEX (OFF)

What do cancer cells look like?

A Bar

Alex, a bartender, stands behind a bar, staring at
Andy. He seems confused and sick for a moment.

ANDY

Well, uh... it's... beautiful, actually.

ALEX

Really? Cancer?

ANDY

Yeah, really.

> *He takes a deep breath, standing up straighter,*
> *and we see the younger, healthier Andy again.*
>
> *He goes to the cabinets and finds a slide, which*
> *he places under the microscope. A blur of*
> *different colors are projected onto the white*
> *wall: blues and reds and purples, pale yellows…*
> *Andy fiddles with a nob and slowly the image*
> *sharpens, until we are looking at a cancer cell.*
> *And it is indeed beautiful. They look for a*
> *moment.*

ALEX

You want a beer?

ANDY

Sure.

> *Andy walks over to the bar. Alex pops a beer and*
> *sets it in front of him.*

ALEX

You a med student?

ANDY

Yeah.

ALEX

We get a lot of you in here. They teach self-medication over
there at Tulane?

ANDY

It's an elective.

ALEX

I bet.
                    (she looks at the image)
So is that the kind of research you do? Cancer?

                         ANDY

That's me.

                         ALEX

What kind of cancer?

                         ANDY
                    (pointing)
That's... me.

                         ALEX

Intense.

                         ANDY

You think?

                         ALEX

So are you gonna be the guy?

                         ANDY

Sorry?

                         ALEX

Who breaks it all open? The guy! The guy who cures--

                         ANDY

Woa, woa, woa! Let's not start talking cures and stuff.

ALEX

Why not? You gotta believe the possibility is there, right?
Otherwise why invest the time? Especially since you might
not have that much time left? Do you? How much?

ANDY

Quite the bedside manner you have.

ALEX

A girl picks up a few things serving you doctors-in-training
all night.

ANDY

Well... let's stay away from the "C" word, okay?

ALEX

Cancer?

ANDY

Cure. I prefer... solution. If you have a...
            (he smiles at the memory)
...a problem.

ALEX

Huh?

ANDY

Sorry. I do a lot of climbing. There's a philosophy that says
that there aren't different routes up a rock, but rather
different problems that need to be solved. If I can gather the
right information, the right data, then maybe I can sneak up
on a solution to my specific problem.

ALEX

What kind you got?

ANDY

Cut right to the chase, don't you?

ALEX

C'mon, what are you working with?

ANDY

Sinonasal Undifferentiated Carcinoma.

ALEX

Never heard of you.

ANDY

Not many have. Pretty rare.

ALEX

Congratulations.

ANDY

Thanks.

ALEX

Wouldn't it be, I don't know, less personally invasive to start by studying one of the big ones?

ANDY

Top forms of cancer: go.

ALEX

Breast.

ANDY

Lung.

ALEX

Brain?

ANDY

Not to mention colon, liver, and bone. Maybe the answer to the big ones is hidden somewhere in my rarer form. Maybe there's a back door somewhere in my cells that nobody has thought to walk through?

ALEX

Maybe. How does it work?

ANDY

What's that?

ALEX

Cancer.

ANDY

It's... it's amazing, actually.
            *(He picks up a marker and begins to diagram on
            the white wall)*
See, normal cells behave in very specific ways. They reproduce themselves exactly and they know when to stop reproducing. They stick together in the correct places and if they are damaged, they self-destruct to make way for healthier cells.
            (He has diagrammed a series of cells.)
But a cancer cell... that's different. A normal cell will reproduce and double itself up to fifty, sixty times and then die. Cancer cells...
            *(He begins to diagram again. At some point it
            grows so large that a projection takes over)*
...they continue to double and double and double. Ordinarily, the body sends out signals and says, you know, "Hey! Knock it off already! That's enough!" But cancer ignores these signals. Like a precocious three year old it says... "Fuck off!" and continues to grow.

ALEX

Quite a mouth your three year old has.

ANDY

All they want to do is go on doubling and growing. And the
more they reproduce with themselves, the more genetic
information in the cell is lost. They get dumber. So
eventually all they know how to do is reproduce until... you
have a tumor.

ALEX

Crazy.

ANDY

And the most important trait?

ALEX

Yeah?

ANDY

They don't die. So, this…
            (looking at the never-ending diagram)
...this goes on forever.

            Beat.

ALEX

Okay, so, and don't take this the wrong way, but... what can
you hope to do in the face of something like that?

ANDY

Seriously, coach, we gotta work on your pep talks.

ALEX

Rah, rah, rah, Go get 'em, team.

ANDY

If we can get the cancer cells to reproduce and grow in the lab, something that's never been done with this type of cancer, then we can study the cell-line and hopefully discover a way to render it non-hostile.

ALEX

Huh. So when you go to work every day, you are literally going to work on yourself.

ANDY

Essentially.

ALEX

Nice to meet you, Mr. Sino...Sinnonase...Mr. Sss--

ANDY

Call me Andy.

ALEX

Will do, Andy. You want a shot?

ANDY

Thanks, but I get enough of those during my treatments.

ALEX

Medical joke. Good one. You want a real shot, Andy?

ANDY

Naw. I should probably get back.

He walks over and finishes his beer.

ALEX

Where is your... where's it live?

ANDY

In my sinuses. My nose.

ALEX

Ouch.

ANDY

Yeah. It's a pain in the ass.

ALEX

An ironic cancer.

ANDY

Good one. It's irritating for the research, because of all the bacteria in the nose. Makes it harder than normal to find cells worth using.

ALEX

Jesus. You sure you don't want a shot?

ANDY

I'm sure.

ALEX

Okay, Mr. Andy. You go get those little fuckers.

ANDY

Yes, ma'am.

A moment listening to the wind and rain.

<u>Lab</u>

The door opens and Kevin enters, arms full of towels and scrubs and various medical sheets.

KEVIN

I had to break a door open, but I got stuff.

*Kevin looks at the water on the floor. He
hesitates, deciding where to put everything, then
settles for randomly dropping piles of sheets in
several places around the floor.*

KEVIN

Whatever, it's a fucking flood.
(going to Andy)
What say you, Dr. Martin?

ANDY

Andy.

KEVIN

And so I say again: what say you, sir?

ANDY

Ready.

KEVIN

Well. Here we go.

*Kevin takes a dramatic swig of his Mountain
Dew. Then he goes to the other side of Andy,
removing the slide from the microscope, and the
projection of the cancer cell vanishes. Kevin
offers a vague, looping sign of the cross over the
microscope. He slips on some medical gloves.
He steps back and gestures to Andy that the
microscope is all his.*

Andy doesn't move.

KEVIN

Dude. You wanted to stay, you might as well look.

ANDY

Yeah.

> *Andy steps to the microscope. Kevin claps hishands together and does a small dance, hopping from foot to foot.*

KEVIN

Movement!

ANDY

Movement is what we want.

KEVIN

Because movement means growth!

ANDY

Growth means life.

KEVIN

And life can be studied!

ANDY

Yes it can. Stop dancing.

KEVIN

Right.

> *Kevin settles. Andy takes a deep breath and bends over the microscope. He takes a slide from the box of tissue cultures and slips it under the microscope. On the wall behind him we see a large, gray, mass. Andy adjusts the focus and the*

mass sharpens. We can see what Andy sees: nothing. The cells are completely still. Dead.

Beat.

Kevin removes the slide and reaches for another. He places it under the microscope.

KEVIN
Here we go slide number two!

Another gray mass appears. Like the first slide, this one is dead. No movement.

Andy steps back, jaw clenched.

Kevin replaces the slide again. He rubs Andy's shoulders like a boxing coach.

KEVIN
Lucky number three, baby.

ANDY
Take your hands off me.

KEVIN
You got it.

Andy bends over and looks. The image sharpens. Nothing. He leans heavily, hands on either side of the microscope.

KEVIN
Fuck!

                         ANDY
              (tense)
It's a process, right?

                         KEVIN
Absolutely! Trial and error.

                         ANDY
Cause and effect.

                         KEVIN
Life and death. Sorry.

                         ANDY
You put in the hours, expect the worst. Gimme another.

              Kevin adds a new slide. Andy looks. Nothing.

                         ANDY
You expect the worst and you persevere. It only takes one.
Right?

                         KEVIN
Right.

                         ANDY
Gimme another.

              Kevin adds a new slide.

                         KEVIN
I mean, any doctor, or scientist, will tell you...

              Andy looks. Nothing.

                         ANDY
Son of a...

62

KEVIN

They'll tell you progress, advances... breakthroughs, you
see, they're made...

ANDY

Gimme another.

Kevin does, Andy looks, nothing.

ANDY

C'mon!

KEVIN

Breakthroughs are made in painstakingly small increments.
Is what they say.

ANDY
Another.
(looks, nothing)
Dammit. Gimme another slide.
(looks)
Nothing. Nothing. There's *nothing*. Gimme another...
(looks)
Fucking why won't you grow?!?!?!

> *By now there is a pile of dead and useless slides.
> Andy sweeps them off the table and they go
> crashing into the back wall. Kevin steps back in
> surprise, as Andy stomps on the slides, breaking
> them apart.*
>
> *There is one slide left that Andy hasn't looked at.
> He and Kevin see it at the same time. Andy
> reaches for it in a rage but Kevin gets there first
> and whips it out of reach.*

KEVIN

Dude!

ANDY

Goddammit!

Andy spins and smacks the wall, hard.

Beat.

KEVIN

Look... maybe the environment wasn't perfect? We can change the media, like you said. Try something new. Maybe shoot for that serum-free method we read about?

ANDY

I don't know.

KEVIN

Andy...

ANDY

I am staring at my own dead cells. Watching them die. I'm getting a preview of the... the nothing that will some day be me.

KEVIN

You're alive now, aren't you?

ANDY

For how long?

There is a loud clap of thunder and suddenly the power blows. The lights go out.

KEVIN
(to the heavens)
Aw, c'mon, really???

> *For a moment all we can hear is the wind and
> the rain. Then there is a click and the backup
> generators kick on. An almost ethereal glow
> emits from the corners of the room.*

KEVIN

Son of a bitch.

> *The door opens and the Chief appears.*

KEVIN

Aw, hey there, Chief.

> *The Chief looks at the microscope and the mess
> on the floor.*

CHIEF
I thought I told you to clear out?

ANDY

I had to see.

CHIEF

And?

ANDY

Nothing.

> *Beat. She nods.*

CHIEF

Let's go.

Kevin goes and stands with the Chief.

KEVIN

I think it's time, buddy. At least the generators kicked on, the freezer should be good for a while.

CHIEF

How many samples are left in there?

ANDY

Thirty.

CHIEF

Okay. That's a good base to start with. *After*. Right?

Andy nods. He goes to the freezer.

ANDY
        (to Kevin)
How's that go again?

KEVIN

Up, down, left, right.

Andy makes a looping sign of the cross over the freezer, then lays his hand on it. He leans his head against it. Then he looks up quickly.

ANDY

Wait.

He looks behind the freezer.

CHIEF

What?

ANDY

The water. It's shorted the freezer.

Kevin moves quickly over.

KEVIN

No juice at all?

ANDY

No.

KEVIN

Is it too late to move it somewhere dry?

ANDY

It's 600 pounds.

KEVIN

I work out.

CHIEF

Once it's shorted, it's out. If we don't open it there should be
enough cold air to keep things stable.

ANDY

But for how long?

CHIEF

I mean...

*Her look says it all. Andy sits down hard in the
water.*

ANDY

All that work.

CHIEF
First things first, let's get you somewhere safe and dry.

ANDY
But--

CHIEF
It's just research. This is your life, Andy.

ANDY
The research *is* my life. You have to know that by now.

CHIEF
I do, but...

She stops as a thought strikes her.

KEVIN
Chief? You kinda stopped talking there.

CHIEF
Nitrogen.

ANDY
What?

CHIEF
Nitrogen!

KEVIN
Are we playing name the elements? Cool. Helium.

CHIEF
There are liquid nitrogen freezers in Dr. Clark's lab across
the way. If we can get the samples from this freezer into one
of those and then get it up a few floors, out of the water,
then...

                        ANDY

How long?

                        CHIEF

Should give us ten days at least.

                        KEVIN

Power has to be on by then, right?

            The Chief moves to the door.

                        CHIEF

We'll have to hope so. Kevin, come give me a hand.

                        KEVIN

On it.

        Kevin follows her. Andy gets shakily to his feet.

                        ANDY

Me too.

                        CHIEF

No, you stay here. You're sick.

                        ANDY

I've been sick for a while.

                        CHIEF

Well, you look sick. Stay here and conserve energy. We'll get
the freezer and then you can help us transfer the samples.
Thirty, you said?

                        ANDY

Yeah.

CHIEF

Good. Let's go.

KEVIN

Sit tight, buddy.

The Chief and Kevin leave. Andy stares after them and then weekly moves to the lab table. He pulls himself up and with effort sits cross-legged on top. He looks at us.

ANDY
(out)

Dear... benefactors?
(not happy with it, but whatever)
Funny. I used to love to sit like this, back in the early days.
When Kevin and I were trying to figure it all out.
(looks down at the water)
The lab was less damp then.

This prompts a little laugh which turns into a coughing fit. As he coughs, the emergency lights flicker and glow brighter. They pulse for a moment, and then go out entirely as the lights in the lab return to normal.

Early Days

Andy sits up straighter, healthier.

Kevin enters with his arms full of papers and bumps into the table.

KEVIN

Ouch.

70

ANDY

Every time.

KEVIN

Are you sure you're not moving the table closer to the door
when I leave?

ANDY

Pretty sure, yeah.

KEVIN

That's gonna leave a mark.

ANDY

Those the new articles?

KEVIN

Yeah. If the Chief catches you sitting on the lab table again...
just saying.

ANDY

Yeah, yeah, yeah. Let me see.
                    Kevin hands Andy the papers.

KEVIN

You check the cultures from last night?

ANDY

Uh-huh.

KEVIN

And?

ANDY

Uh-uh.

KEVIN

Damn. I thought that was a good mixture, too.

ANDY

They were fibroblasted all to shit.

KEVIN

Really???

ANDY

Would I lie to you, Kevin?

KEVIN

I mean, I like to think we have something special here, but in my experience just when you think that connection is headed to the next--

ANDY

That was rhetorical.

KEVIN

Right. Gotcha.
                (Beat. He fidgets while Andy reads)
How long do you have to wait to do another excision?

ANDY

I'd rather avoid that, if it's possible.

KEVIN

I don't know why, I mean, it's only like, an 18 inch needle inserted right into your nasal cavity.

ANDY

I remember, I was there.

                          KEVIN

Right.
                  (small beat, then...)
Oh!

                  Andy jumps, startled.

                          ANDY

...yes?

                          KEVIN

Glow-in-the-dark-mice!

                          ANDY

I don't...

                          KEVIN

Glow-in-the-dark-mice!

                          ANDY
How much Mountain Dew have you had today?

                  *Kevin takes the stack of papers and starts
                  flipping through them.*

                          KEVIN
I knew I should have left it on top so I'd remember. I was
reading through it last night, and... ah-ha!
                  *(he finds what he's looking for and hands it to
                  Andy)*
So, this lab in... uh, wherever, Hopkins, maybe? I'm sure it's
in there somewhere. Anyway, they were trying to grow
tumors like us, except for breast cancer research, and they
added irradiated mouse cells to the culture. The mouse cells
were still alive but unable to grow and essentially they acted
as food for the cancer cells. And *that*--

ANDY

You see me reading it, right?

KEVIN

Yeah, yeah. Cool, right?

ANDY

Interesting, that's for sure.

KEVIN

Feed the beast, you know?

ANDY

Chief will love it when we ask for glow-in-the-dark mice.

KEVIN

Oh, can I ask her, please? She loves me.

ANDY

Sure about that?

KEVIN

Yeah... you should ask her.

ANDY

Thanks.

KEVIN

But I'm making progress. I will win her over.

Andy gets off the table, thinking out loud.

ANDY

So. We add irradiated mouse cells to the FBS serum we're already using as a base.

KEVIN

Maybe up the RPMI 1640?

ANDY

All that sugar combined with the new food source...

KEVIN

I mean... how many did we lose from the last batch?

ANDY

All fifteen.

KEVIN

So...?

ANDY

Not like we can do worse, right?

KEVIN

Exactly.

The Chief enters. She is holding a bottle of port.

CHIEF

Gentlemen. How goes it?

KEVIN
(trying too hard)
It goeth well, most learned Chief Tyler.

CHIEF

It's... Cameron?

KEVIN

Kevin.

                          CHIEF
Right.

                    Awkward beat, Kevin smiling really wide and
                    staring.

                          CHIEF
Right.
                    (turns to Andy)
How did it go with the last batch?

                          ANDY
Not so good. We lost them all.

                          KEVIN
No bueno.

                          CHIEF
Well, we knew it would be a tough road. With so many
ingredients, it's difficult to know which macromolecules the
cells need to thrive. How are you holding up physically?

                          ANDY
Fine.

                          CHIEF
Mentally?

                          ANDY
I'm fine. We were thinking of maybe trying a serum-free
media, and Kevin found this really interesting article--

                          KEVIN
Can we have glow-in-the-dark-mice???

                          CHIEF
I'm sorry?

76

ANDY

I'll send you a copy of the article. It would be a long shot,
but maybe down the road.

CHIEF

Sounds good.

Kevin points at the port.

KEVIN

Whatcha got there, Chief?

CHIEF

Yes. I got this for you.

KEVIN

Aw, you shouldn't have.

CHIEF

For Andy.

KEVIN

Naturally.

ANDY

Is that...?

CHIEF

It's port. I know you're a wine buff, but I think you're really
going to love this.

She hands it to Andy.

ANDY
(reading the label)
"Fonseca 1994 Vintage." Port, huh?

CHIEF

Really good port.

ANDY

What's the occasion?

CHIEF

A, uh... a celebration bottle, let's say.

ANDY

What are we celebrating?

CHIEF

Nothing. Yet. But...

> *She stops. They can tell there is something wrong.*

ANDY

What's going on?

CHIEF

Well, the thing is... you see...

KEVIN

Jeez, Chief, spit it out, we study cancer, you know? How bad could it--
> *(stops himself when he sees her glaring at him)*

Sorry.
> *Beat.*

CHIEF

Andy, we've run out of money.

ANDY

Wait, what? What do you mean? I thought--

CHIEF

There was $20,000 allotted for your use, paid from the
school's discretionary funds.

ANDY

Right.

CHIEF

This type of research is expensive, Andy. All of the
equipment, the gathering of the cells from your sinuses, the
various serums, Cameron's radioactive hamsters... it adds up.

KEVIN

They're mice, and it's Kevin, but it doesn't matter and I see
your point.

ANDY

Are you saying that this last round, this round that yielded
nothing, was *literally* the last round?

CHIEF

I'm saying if you--if we--want to continue with this research,
then we need to figure out how to finance it.

ANDY

And you brought me a bottle of port to soften the blow?

CHIEF

I brought the port to remind you that I still believe there will
be something to celebrate. And to soften the blow, yes.

KEVIN

Didn't have any Mountain Dew, huh?

She ignores Kevin.

CHIEF

Look, Andy, this is how it goes. Medical research is a
continuing loop of securing funds to pay for trials that lead
to breakthroughs that require more funds. All that's
happened is we've reached the point where one round of
trials is complete, and now we need the money to pay for the
next round.

ANDY

I know, I'm sorry, I didn't mean to... you know.

CHIEF

Of course.

ANDY

I don't suppose you have any ideas on where to find more
money?

CHIEF

Well, there are the usual channels--

ANDY

Come on, Chief Tyler, grant applications take time! I have
ideas now. I need to be able to see this through.

CHIEF

I understand that, Andy, which is why--

KEVIN
(blurts)
What if we broke a World Record?

Beat. They look at him.

KEVIN

Okay, bear with me, it's actually not as crazy as it sounds.

ANDY

Kev, I don't think this is the--

KEVIN

This is exactly the time! Right?! I mean, we're out of money, we need more money, we need to raise funds fast, a, uh... a fundraiser, if you will, so...

ANDY

So we break a World Record?

KEVIN

Sure.

CHIEF

(to Andy)

How do you manage to get any work done in here?

KEVIN

Yeah, Chief, ha-ha, "Cameron's so funny" *whatever*. Look: you're real busy running the School of Medicine and all, and Andy locks himself away in this lab, but if either of you spent any time on campus, amongst the people--

CHIEF

I'm not sure what...

KEVIN

--then what you would know is that *people like Andy*. They do. They are rooting for him. They think what he's doing is brave, and selfless, and if *f* do I'm pretty sure the rest of the community will also, and if we stage something cool that would bring a lot of people together, then maybe... you know. Cha-ching.

Beat. A smile from the Chief? She considers.

CHIEF
You might actually be on to something, Cameron.

KEVIN
Kevin.

CHIEF
Right.

She holds her hand out to Andy for the port.

ANDY
You're taking it back already?

CHIEF
When you brought the idea for this research to me, I thought... well, I thought it was unrealistic. Given your circumstances.

ANDY
Yeah, I know, but...

CHIEF
No, no. You convinced me. And you justified my allowing you to do this research. You continue to justify it by doing good work. And much as your assistant here thinks I live with my head up a test tube, I also can see how your peers have responded. So...

She holds out her hand again, and Andy gives her back the bottle.

ANDY
Really good port.

CHIEF
Exactly. Which we will drink together in celebration. Later.

ANDY

Fingers crossed.

CHIEF
(She considers him)
What would winning be for you, Andy?

ANDY

I'd kinda like my hair back.

CHIEF

You're not going to find a cure. You knew that going in,
right?

ANDY

Chief...

CHIEF

The research is what's most important. The steps you take in
here could open up pathways that other people hadn't
thought to walk down. It's about discovery, it's about pushing
forward. It's about fighting. Finding growth from cells bent
on destroying you, even if--

ANDY

Even if I'm not the one that benefits from that growth.

The Chief nods.

CHIEF

I look forward to drinking this with you.

KEVIN

Both of us, right Chief?

CHIEF

Find us a world record we can break quickly, and I'll
consider it.

KEVIN

Yes ma'am!

CHIEF

And you'll of course forgive me if I continue to seek out
grants and benevolent donors in the meantime.

KEVIN

No offense taken at all.

> *The Chief walks to the cabinets. She takes a key
> from her pocket and unlocks one of them. She
> places the bottle of port inside, then locks it up
> and puts the key back in her pocket.*

ANDY

Aw! Not fair.

CHIEF

I giveth and I taketh away. Let's get it done, gentlemen.
Onward!

> *Chief leaves.*

KEVIN

Well, I think that was a big step for her and me. Real
connection.

ANDY

Whatever you say... Cameron.

KEVIN

Hey, if she needs me to be Cameron, I am happy to oblige.
Okay. Lots to do. I need a list of all records breakable by
nerdy medical researchers. But first I need caffeine. You
want?

ANDY

I'm okay.

KEVIN

Cool. Be right back.

> *Kevin exits.*

> *The lights flicker again, and Andy looks around,
> confused. Then there is a clap of thunder and the
> emergency lights return.*

ANDY

Dear Adjudicators of the Guinness World Records
Committee… HA! We did it! Don't ask me how, but Kevin
lit a fire, and...

Okay, in a nutshell... during a brainstorming session Kevin
remarked that he had seen the Chief jogging around campus.
Chief let on that she has been an avid runner for ages, and
that she has done several marathons, and ultra marathons,
and then Kevin consulted the Guinness Bible, and... turns out
there is a World Record for the "Longest Distance Run
While Dribbling a Basketball Over a 24-Hour Period." It
took a little convincing, but... I love Kevin. His energy is
boundless. He canvased this campus, this town, we took
pledges, raised money... and then one Sunday morning at
9:30am Chief Tyler started jogging around the Tulane
University Track while dribbling a basketball signed by the
entire Oncology Department. My classmates showed up and
took turns running next to her. They would keep her

company, pass her bottles of water and slices of pizza. There
was a marching band practicing that afternoon, and they
played "You'll Never Walk Alone". I would've preferred
"Walk This Way", or maybe "Running on Empty", but hey.
She was... it was such a thing to watch. I couldn't believe...
y'know, for me... that she would...
>   *(beat)*
She had three hours to go and developed tendonitis in her
right elbow, from all the dribbling. So... she *switched hands!*
She ran the last three hours using her left hand, and when all
was said and done she had run 108 miles. We raised $28,000
in donations, which was enough to fund one more round of
cell cultures. 108 miles.
>   *(beat)*
And where did it get us? A once-in-a-generation storm, a
freezer full of my tissue, and a lab on the cusp of flooding.

> *Andy slouches, sicker again, coughing. He looks
> at us.*

Back when SNUC resurfaced the second time, I went a
little... crazy. Couldn't decide what the best... which problem
to tackle. And how to tackle them. I had some fantasies
about just being out in the world. On a rock. In the
mountains. Or on a surfboard out in the ocean.

> *Emergency lights flicker again.*

A Coffee Shop

> *Hannah walks from behind the white wall. She
> sets a stool down at the end of the table and sits.
> She has two coffee cups and hands one to Andy.*

HANNAH

You wanna do what?

ANDY

C'mon, sis.

HANNAH

No, please. Explain it to me.

ANDY

I just want to get away.

HANNAH

Look, I get the desire. And I can empathize. I went freaking camping with you.

ANDY

Yes, you did.

HANNAH

And I did not cut and run on that stupid--

ANDY

Beautiful.

HANNAH

--big ass piece of rock you dragged me up. But, now...

ANDY

I'm sorry, are you equating your camping trip with my cancer?

HANNAH

Of course not. But--

ANDY

What?

HANNAH

Things are different. Right? There's... there's a deadline now.
And you wanna spend your final days on this earth surfing?

ANDY

Why not? I always wanted to try it, and this could be the
perfect chance.

HANNAH

Are you kidding me?

ANDY

You got a better idea?

HANNAH

I feel like *any* idea would be better.

ANDY

So name one.

HANNAH

I mean... you could... dammit, Andy, you're my little brother!
I want you to do something, *anything* besides just checking
out.

ANDY

I'm not checking out, I'm just—

HANNAH

What?

ANDY

I'm escaping.

HANNAH

That's not your only option. There's still--

ANDY

What, chemo? Again?

HANNAH

For starters.

ANDY

To what end?

HANNAH

Andy--

ANDY

Seriously. It didn't work the first time. Only half of my doctors have even heard of SNUC. We'd literally be throwing various treatments at my disease in the hopes that one of them would work.

HANNAH

That's better than nothing.

ANDY

Better than carving a bottom turn?

HANNAH

Excuse me?

ANDY

Better than cutting a perfect line down a cresting wave and pulling out on the shoulder just before it closes out?

HANNAH

Are you just making up words?

ANDY

I read about it in a surfing magazine.

HANNAH

C'mon, Andy.

ANDY

Tell me it doesn't sound... *gnarly*.

Beat.

HANNAH

Andy, you can't give up.

ANDY

I'm not. But I need... I need to face it my own way.

HANNAH

What about school?

ANDY

I can still go back.

HANNAH

I mean, you wanted to be a doctor.

ANDY

I know. But I feel like if I went I'd spend most of my time skipping Organic Chem to go climbing.

HANNAH

Maybe you owe it to yourself--

ANDY

What good would getting a medical degree do me?

HANNAH

You don't know what's going to happen!

ANDY

Neither do you! Or mom. Or dad, or anybody. I'm the one living with this thing and I'm the one that's going to die from it!

HANNAH

People live with cancer all the time, Andy.

ANDY

It's not just cancer! Why do I have to keep saying that?! This is something different. Smarter. Worse.

HANNAH

So we're supposed to just throw up our hands and give you space?!

ANDY

I mean... yes!

HANNAH

Fuck you.

ANDY

C'mon--

HANNAH

No, really, fuck you. You're my brother and I love you. And I know that you're too smart to believe all that crap you're trying to sell yourself. Climbing, surfing--

ANDY

It's not crap.

HANNAH
(bad Keanu Reeves impression)

"I'm gonna surf, sis. I'm totally gonna seek out the perfect set and ride a tubular board down a radical... fucking... pipeline of awesomeness."

Beat.

ANDY

Sorry, who's voice is that?

HANNAH

That was me being you being Keanu Reeves in *Point Break.*

ANDY

Nice.

HANNAH

Whatever.
(beat)
The point, Andy, is that ever since you were little you were... active. You know? Involved. All these ideas... don't direct your energy away from this fight you have. Channel it. Inward. Don't let this fucking disease make you sit back. Go after it.

He thinks about this.

ANDY

So, you think--

The lights flicker. Hannah stands up and barks at Andy, as the Chief.

CHIEF

I'm sorry, Mr. Martin, you wanna do what?

Andy looks confused. The Chief crosses to the other side of Andy where an office desk has emerged. She puts on a white doctor's coat and sits. Andy turns to face her.

Office

ANDY

Uh... call me, Andy, please.

CHIEF

Very well. Andy.

ANDY

Thank you for taking the time to meet with me, Chief Tyler. You read my proposal?

CHIEF

I did.

Another small flicker. Andy hops off the lab table and joins the Chief in her office.

ANDY

Well, like I stated--

CHIEF

Yes, indeed.

ANDY

I think that the time is right for just this kind of project. Tulane Medical Center enjoys a sterling reputation for research as well as care--

CHIEF

Andy.

ANDY

Not to mention that this is a teaching hospital, and I am, as you know--

CHIEF

I do.

ANDY

A student. So, like I said... the time is right.

CHIEF

No.

ANDY

I'm sorry?

CHIEF

Hell no!

ANDY

Chief Tyler--

CHIEF

Look, Andy, I'm not indifferent to the rather personal nature of your motivation, but the simple truth is that we don't do this kind of research here at Tulane.

ANDY

Yes ma'am, I understand that. But surely as the Chief of Hematology and Medical Oncology, you are precisely the person who can change that.

CHIEF

Technically speaking, yes. But--

ANDY

You, here in your labs, have successfully grown ovarian
cancer tumors using tissue donated by patients.

CHIEF

Yes.

ANDY
(spreading his arms wide)
I'm just another patient willing and wanting to donate tissue.

CHIEF

Yes, but you're not just another patient, are you? You're also
proposing to be the doctor in charge of researching that
tissue. Your tissue.

ANDY

Who could know me better than me?

CHIEF

What about objectivity? If you don't find the answers you are
looking for, how will you be able to maintain the
professional distance necessary to analyze the results that
you do get?

ANDY

I would argue that professional distance can be just as much
to blame when it comes to objectivity. I don't want to be
objective. I want to fight! Why do the doctors get to be the
ones doing all the fighting? All that's left for the patients to
fight is side effects!

CHIEF

You don't have the experience for this kind of research.

ANDY

This is how I get it.

CHIEF
And we don't have the resources right now.

ANDY
I'll work alone, maybe with just one assistant, a fellow student. We'll have fund raisers!

CHIEF
I just don't think--

ANDY
Look, Chief, this is--quite literally--my life.

Beat. The Chief sits back. Andy notices a series of framed pictures on her desk. He looks closely at one.

ANDY
You run marathons?

CHIEF
Yes. But that particular photo is from an ultra-marathon.

ANDY
What's the difference?

CHIEF
Ultras are extended marathons. Longer.

ANDY
Why?

CHIEF
(shrugging)

Why not?

ANDY

So, when you say "extended," I mean, how long is that?

CHIEF

They vary. Some are specific lengths above and beyond the traditional 26 miles, and some are a set time that you run and see how far you can get.

ANDY

What's the farthest you've gone?

CHIEF

125 miles.

ANDY

Dear God!

CHIEF

I find it invigorating.

ANDY

I imagine you would have to. How do you manage to keepgoing? I mean, after mile five I would be tapping out, much less mile 125.

CHIEF

Sometimes you just have to will yourself to stay in the race.

ANDY

One foot in front of the other?

CHIEF

Exactly.

> *Beat.*

ANDY

My first round of treatment, I had utter faith in my doctors.
The second time through, I had utter faith that I was both
better and smarter than them. And I thought at the time that
surely there had to be people somewhere who had training
and knowledge that would help me.

CHIEF

And that's what brought you here, to my office?

ANDY

We are all so fallible. So less than perfect. So... impotent
despite all of our abilities. There are only 100 documented
cases of my kind of cancer.

CHIEF

Yes.

ANDY

Carrying with it a 100% mortality rate within five years of
diagnoses.

CHIEF

I know.

ANDY

Not to mention, SNUC cells have never been cultured.
Nobody else is looking into this. If I don't study it, who will?
I'm literally running my own marathon against my body. And
it's not one I have any illusions about finishing, but... I have
to stay in the race, right?

CHIEF

Andy, have you ever thought that maybe, with the time you
have left, you could--

ANDY

Go surfing and resign myself to my fate?

CHIEF

Spend time with your family?

ANDY

Spending time with my family is what convinced me to do this.

CHIEF

I see.

ANDY

Things to do when you get diagnosed with cancer: go.

CHIEF

I'm sorry?

ANDY

Never mind. Look, Chief, I would rather sidestep the clinical duties of a typical third year student and instead do the type of research that will further our understanding of SNUC. Maybe this research will lead to something that will help people who are diagnosed with SNUC in the future.
          (beat)
If this cancer is going to get me, it can damn sure expect a fight.

CHIEF

The cancer resides in your sinus cavity. Behind your eyes. Near your brain. In order to get usable samples of tissue we would have to cut into your head.

ANDY

Step ahead of you, Chief. I've already spoken with doctors Ballantine and Demers--

CHIEF

Of course you have.

ANDY

And they think they can get tissue from my tumor by
inserting a needle directly into my sinuses. It's less invasive
and we can do it right in their office.

CHIEF

Well, then.

ANDY

And because it's my tumor we don't need Institutional
Review Board approval. So we can start as soon as we like.
Tomorrow, even.

CHIEF

Andy.

ANDY

Hypothetically, of course.
(beat)
Let me fight this. Please. Didn't someone long ago say,
"Physician, heal thyself."

> The Chief nods, and smiles. Then the emergency
> lights flicker. She stands slowly and points at
> Andy.

CHIEF

Better get to work, Mr. Martin.

> Andy shudders, dizzy, as if he might fall. He
> shakes his head to clear it and jumps back into
> the lab. Weakly, he manages to revert to his
> cross-legged position on the table.

<u>Lab</u>

The sound of the storm.

ANDY

(to us)

Dear... dear friends. I, uh... I've always found the sounds of a storm to be soothing. Any time we had bad weather growing up, my mother and I would grab blankets and sit on the front porch, listening to the wind and the rain.

(he closes his eyes to listen)

I keep replaying all these conversations, all these moments that have led me to where I am right now. But I can't keep straight... it's like I don't remember exactly who said what. Or when. It's almost like it's all variations on the same person, bombarding me... millions of tiny drops of water crashing onto my head at once.

Andy's head drops into his hands, as sick and weak as we've seen him.

The door opens and Kevin is there with the Chief. There is a heavy-looking mini-freezer between them.

KEVIN

Okay, we got it.

(trying to maneuver the freezer through the doorway)

Holy crap. Could this thing be any heavier?

CHIEF

Maybe you don't work out as much as you should.

KEVIN

The ladies like me lean.

They manage to get the freezer into the room.
They move it down to the end of the table near
the bigger freezer. They pause to catch their
breath.

CHIEF

This is a portable liquid nitrogen freezer. If we can transfer
the remaining cultures into this it should buy us enough time.

ANDY

Ten days?

The Chief nods, face set. Andy gets off the table,
and the three line up. Kevin by the large freezer,
the Chief at the smaller, and Andy in the middle.
Kevin and the Chief look at Andy.

CHIEF

Ready?

Kevin nods and holds a fist straight out. They
look at him.

KEVIN

What? I thought we were gonna have a sports ball-type
moment-thing.

Andy smiles and weakly fist-bumps Kevin. They
look at the Chief.

CHIEF

Okay. On three. One... two... three.

They get to work. Kevin opens the large freezer
and carefully removes a tray of samples. He
passes it to Andy, who turns to the Chief. She

*opens the small freezer and a hiss of cold air
and steam is released. Andy quickly lays the tray
inside the small freezer. They repeat the process
for the second tray of samples, and then the
third. After the final tray is inside the freezer, the
Chief slams the lid shut and locks it. Andy kneels
down and gently lays a hand on the lid of the
freezer, almost a caress. The Chief, in turn, puts
a hand on Andy's shoulder.*

CHIEF

Stay in the race.

ANDY

One foot at a time?

CHIEF

Exactly. Okay, we have to keep this out of the water.

*A series of blocks or platforms create a kind of
staircase. The three roll the freezer over to the
lowest step, and struggle to lift it up.*

*As they do, there is a roar from the storm and
the door to the lab bursts open as a wave of
water rushes in. (I know, I know. I have no doubt
this can be achieved in whatever technical way
makes sense, via sound, light and projections.
That said, it would be really cool to see the stage
flood.)*

They turn and look at the incoming water.

KEVIN

Jesus Christ, what next?

CHIEF

Keep moving! Up as high as we can get it!

> *They move the freezer to the next step and begin
> to lift it. Andy loses his grip and his knees
> buckle.*

KEVIN

Woa, buddy.

ANDY

Sorry.

KEVIN

Maybe you should let us do this.

ANDY

They're my cells.

CHIEF

Kevin's right.

KEVIN

I'll remember you said that.

CHIEF

Andy, you're weak. Let us take care of it.

ANDY

No! They're mine, they're me.

> *With effort, Andy stands back up and gives the
> freezer a push. Together, they manage to get it
> up onto the second step. They pause, breathing
> heavy.*

KEVIN

One more floor?

CHIEF

One more should do it.

Andy nods. He gets back to his feet and they prepare to push/lift the freezer onto the last step.

KEVIN

And... *PUSH.*

The three push the freezer up onto the last step. The force of the push brings Andy to his knees again, leaning on the freezer.

A roar from the storm. The emergency lights flicker and glow. Kevin and the Chief step away from Andy. They put their arms around each other and look back at him.

MOM

Honey, are you sure?

ANDY

I think so, Mom.

DAD

C'mon, Andy...

MOM

Sweetheart, it's his decision.

DAD

Like hell it is.

ANDY

Dad, I think I have to do this.

DAD

Yes, you've made that clear.

MOM

It's not worth fighting about.

DAD

Well, why not?

ANDY

This is important.

DAD

More important than your family?

ANDY

Nothing's more important than that. Don't take it--

DAD

How else are we supposed to take it?

MOM

I think it's brave.

DAD

Oh, really?

MOM

I do.

DAD

You think it's brave to completely shut your family out of what could be the only fight you have left in your life?

MOM

(overlapping on "out")

I think it's brave to want to fight at all! I think--

ANDY

Well, you tell me! If I sit back, I'm a coward. If I go to school and research I'm abandoning my family. You tell me what the right decision is, and I'll make it.

DAD

Don't make me out to be--

MOM

I think I am very proud of him and I think that you are too because this is who we raised him to be.

Beat.

ANDY

I just feel like, with the resources I have there... I'll be able to do some good. Research like this could be important.

DAD

(a little desperate)

What about travel?

ANDY

Yeah...

DAD

You were gonna use some of... you were going to see the world. Surf! Hell, I'll come with you.

ANDY

That sounds great.

DAD

Absolutely. Say the word, Andy, and I'll get the tickets right now. For all of us. Three tickets, first class, round trip around the world.

MOM

If you're flying around the world, wouldn't you only need the ticket to be one way?

Beat.

DAD

I just... I hate to think of you stuck inside a lab.

ANDY

I'm not gonna be a hamster, Dad. I'll be in charge.

DAD

Experimenting on the hamsters.

ANDY

Maybe I'll make them glow in the dark.

A flicker from the emergency lights.

MOM

What?

ANDY

Sorry. Nothing. I don't know...

MOM

Whatever you feel you need to do, we'll support you. Your father just has trouble sometimes with things that he can't control.

ANDY

Must be where I get it.

> *Andy slumps, exhausted. The lights flicker.*
> *Thunder. Dad turns to Andy, his tone changing,*
> *becoming cold.*

DAD

Look at you. Wasting away.

ANDY

(confused)
Wait, no. You never said that.

MOM

(cold)
How do you know?

ANDY

Um...

DAD

How do you know anything anymore? You're sick.

MOM

How many rounds of chemo?

DAD

Too many.

ANDY

I'm close...

DAD

Close to what?

                    ANDY
We're almost there, the end.

                    DAD
Of?

                    MOM
Will it be enough?

                    ANDY
No, this last batch...

                    DAD
Andy.

                    ANDY
This could be the last batch...

                    DAD
Andy. This is the fight you've chosen.

                    MOM
And it's only going to get worse.

                    ANDY
I know, but...

            *Sounds of the storm. Dad suddenly becomes one
            of the many doctors Andy has encountered.*

                    DOCTOR
I'm sorry to say, Mr. Martin--

                    ANDY
            (weak)
Please call me Andy.

DOCTOR

This next round of radiation is not going to be pleasant.

ANDY

Up to now it's been a blast.

DOCTOR

You can expect ulcers, most likely on the inside of the mouth.

ANDY

Will I be able to speak?

DOCTOR

You'll have the ability, but it will be painful.

ANDY

Ulcers.

DOCTOR

Sores. Open and oozing.

ANDY

What about my sense of taste?

DOCTOR

We'll have to wait and see, but it will likely be affected as well.

ANDY

So much for wine.

DOCTOR

I doubt you'll have the desire to eat or drink anything at all.

Mom lays a hand on Andy's shoulder.

MOM

Honey?

ANDY

I'm pretty tired, Mom. I can't... which problem first? It's starting to all blur together.

>*Mom becomes the Chief, and she and the Doctor*
>*flank Andy.*

CHIEF

Sinonasal Undifferentiated Carcinoma, Mr. Martin.

ANDY

My little fuckers.

CHIEF

We do not do this type of research at this facility.

ANDY

But...

DOCTOR

Sinonasal.

CHIEF

You'll be too weak.

DOCTOR

Undifferentiated.

CHIEF

How can you expect to be both patient and doctor?

DOCTOR

Carcinoma.

112

CHIEF

You won't have the strength.

DOCTOR

SNUC.

CHIEF

We don't have the funds--

DOCTOR

Tumors.

CHIEF

For this type of research, for this type of--

DOCTOR

Cancer.

CHIEF

Cancer.

Fast and overlapping.

DOCTOR

Insidious.

CHIEF

Hiding.

DOCTOR

Attacking.

CHIEF

Cancer.

DOCTOR

Cancer.

CHIEF/DOCTOR

Cancer!!!

ANDY

STOP!!!

The Doctor tears off his white coat, becoming Kevin.

KEVIN

Hey buddy. Things worth living for: go!

There is a loud roar from the storm. The emergency lights flicker, shine bright for a second, and then it all drops away.

Andy alone in the silence. Behind him, on the white wall, a brilliant setting sun appears, sinking towards the horizon.

ANDY

Climbing. Mountains. Sunsets. Have you ever watched the sun set from the side of a mountain? It is quite a thing. Like a reward for the work it took to make it to the top. A brilliant gold medal that morphs to orange, red, violet... colors in between that you wouldn't dare dream existed. That you could spend your entire life trying to recreate on canvas, reaching for just the right brush, just the right paint. Pablo Picasso once said, "Everything you can imagine is real."

Andy looks up at the setting sun. Mixed into the colors of the sunset is the line of cells Andy diagrammed earlier. He reaches up and finds a handhold on the wall, and begins to climb. Each new handhold and foothold mapped out by the cell diagram. He makes his way up and across

the wall towards the very top corner, and the
sun.
As he climbs...

ANDY (CONT)

Doctors, researchers of disease... in the lab I've always felt that we are like painters. We start with a canvas, a cell, a dish. And we decide color, shape, texture, line, image. We create. And if we have to resurrect Picasso to facilitate this process, we will. We imagine, we believe that the results are out there waiting to be discovered, to be made real. Once these cells can be reliably grown, with or without me to do it, we can learn how they behave and then how to eliminate them. One step at a time, chasing sunset after sunset until finally, I, you, we... reach the summit and can at long last look out and see that that distant horizon is, impossibly, closer. More real.

> *Andy has reached the top of the wall. He holds*
> *on by two feet and one hand. The next, final*
> *handhold is just out of reach.*

Fucking deadpoints.

> *He steadies himself, and then pushes up,*
> *reaching. He grabs the top of the wall and pulls*
> *himself up to sit, staring out.*
>
> *Below him, the sun sets.*
>
> *The lab and everything else fades away and*
> *Andy sits in a small pool of peaceful light.*

I'm tired. I'm... losing. I... am, I said.
            (beat. He sings softly)
"I am, I said. To no one there. I am, I cried. And I am lost and I don't even know why."

(beat)

ANDY (CONT)

I have another round of chemo coming up. The doctors tell me that there is the possibility that the radiation will leave me blind. No more sunsets.
(beat)
There are so many people I want to keep fighting for. My parents, the Chief, Kevin. All the patients waging their own, similar, private wars. It's just so hard. At this point all I am equipped with is the viable hope that someone, somewhere, will not rest until this disease is brought under control. Even if that someone is not me.
(beat)
You spend enough time climbing, bouldering, solving problems, working your way around, across and up these majestic piles of rock... it's hard not to wonder... What would it feel like? To become... untethered. To fall. To stare down one final deadpoint. To know that the last handhold is right there, but maybe too far? But still... to know you have to try. So you reach. You push, you surge upward and then comes that moment when you stop rising and just hang there between two realities. Either your fingers catch hold or gravity takes over. A quick moment of panic, a surge of adrenaline, and then... just you and the air.
(beat)
Given how much pain there is in this world, would it be a relief? The moment would be quick, but how long would it feel? Could you live another lifetime in that moment of peaceful falling?
(beat)
There are so many mountains I didn't climb.He closes his eyes and spreads his arms wide.

Silently, he falls backward, over the wall and out of sight.

116

A long silence.

The door to the lab opens and we see the silhouette of a man. He stands in the doorway for a second and then steps into the lab. The door closes behind him, returning us to darkness.

In the dark, we hear the man take a few steps and then bump into the table.

                         KEVIN
Ouch! Shit.

He fumbles in the dark and then flips the light switch. Bright, stark light illuminates the lab.

Kevin stands there, holding an industrial-looking lunchbox.

The lab is a mess, as they left it.

Kevin raises his hand against the light, and then uses the dimmer switch to lower the lights to a more intimate glow. He sets the lunchbox on the table. He takes out matches and lights the candles.

Carefully he opens the lunchbox. He puts on gloves and removes a slide. He places the slide under the microscope and takes a step back. He makes a large, swooping sign of the cross.

He flips a switch and behind him we see the familiar, vague blur.

He takes a deep breath and leans over, looking into the microscope and fiddling with the focus.

Behind him the image sharpens. Slowly, we can see that--unlike all the others--this dish contains healthy tumor cells which are moving and reproducing.

Kevin lets out a yell of surprise and takes a step back. He takes another look.

                    KEVIN
Ha!! You... little... fuckers.
          (he does a little dance, then stops, overcome.)
Way to go, Andy.

In the doorway, the Chief appears. She stands there, watching, until Kevin realizes she's there.

                    KEVIN
Oh, hey Chief.

Kevin gestures at the microscope and the wall, smiling wide. The Chief nods, taking it in. Then she takes a key from her pocket and goes to the cabinet, unlocking it and taking out the port.

Andy steps from behind the white wall, leaning against it and looking healthy and vibrant. He watches as the Chief opens the bottle and pours two small glasses. She gives one to Kevin. He smells the port, then holds the glass up in a toast. The Chief clinks with him and they both take a sip.

The Chief smiles, happy. Kevin grimaces, choking.

Andy laughs.

                    KEVIN

No. Nope. Can' do it.

            He retrieves a Mountain Dew from the mini-
            fridge and takes a huge sip.

                    CHIEF

Better?

                    KEVIN

Oh yeah.

            Kevin suddenly gives her a huge hug. She allows
            it, and maybe even smiles. Kevin holds it for an
            awkward amount of time.

                    CHIEF

Kevin?

                    KEVIN

Yes, Chief?

                    CHIEF

Let me go.

                    KEVIN

Sorry, Chief.

            He lets go. The two of them look a the cells
            moving on the white wall.

                    CHIEF

Okay, then. Onward.

            She exits.

Kevin takes another look and then realizes...

KEVIN
Holy crap! I gotta... we gotta call people! Hey, Chief!
(yelling out the door)
Chief!!! We gotta make some calls!!

CHIEF (OFF)
Yes, Kevin, I know.

Kevin exits after her.

KEVIN
Ha! I knew it! I knew I was making progress...

Andy is alone in the lab. He goes to Kevin's unfinished glass of port and holds it up against the candle light. He swirls it, smells, takes a sip, and it might very well be the best thing he's ever tasted. He turns to look at the cells moving around on the white board.

He lifts his glass to us in a salute, and takes another sip. He takes one more look at the cells moving behind him, then leans over and blows out the candles.

Darkness.

THE END